PATHWAYS TO THE

CW00968367

ALONG THE
Mohawk Trail

A Feast of Fall Foliage and Spectacular Hill Towns

By David J. McLaughlin and Laren Bright

Photographs by
Jim McElholm and David J. McLaughlin

Along the Mohawk Trail: A Feast of Fall Foliage and Spectacular Hill Towns

First print edition 2006

No part of this publication may be reproduced by any mechanical, photographic or electronic process or in the form of a photographic recording, nor may it be stored in a retrieval system, transmitted or otherwise copied for public or private use without prior written permission from the publisher.

Library of Congress Control Number: 2005900540
ISBN 0-9763500-2-5
SAN 255-4860

For further information on this publication and related Pathways to the Past products, visit our website at www.pentacle-press.com.

To contact the publisher write:

Pentacle Press
P.O. Box 9400
Scottsdale, AZ 85252
sales@pentacle-press.com

Printed in Hong Kong

GETTING THE MOST FROM THIS GUIDE

The Mohawk Trail is one of the oldest scenic routes in New England. It combines charming vestiges of early 20th-century touring, when the Model-T cars had trouble navigating the steep trail, with newer attractions such as the Great Falls Discovery Center in Turners Falls and MASS MoCA in North Adams.

This guide has been organized to show you all of these attractions and many more in the often bypassed hill towns above and below the Trail. As a result, although the guide is organized in a generally linear fashion going from east to west, we include a number of "side journeys" that will take you from and back to the Trail.

At the back of the guide are listings of resources, places to stay and references. Consult them to help you plan your trip, and keep in mind the following tips:

- There are motels and bed-and-breakfasts all along Route 2, and even a few vintage cabins. Upscale accommodations in the region are limited. Reservations are essential during the foliage season (mid-September to mid-October) and many summer weekends.

- We show you all the central routes, but this area is made for wandering back-country roads. We highly recommend that you acquire maps that show all the town roads.

- Check for county fairs, craft shows, concerts and other special activities using the Internet links and phone numbers provided.

- The Mohawk Trail region is a natural water wonderland. Try to fit in a kayak or raft trip or a fishing expedition. Or simply get out of the car a few times and hike in the region's plentiful forests.

All in all, we hope you find *Along the Mohawk Trail* both a useful resource in planning and navigating your trip and a wonderful visual memento of this unique part of our country.

TABLE OF
Contents

HISTORY OF THE
Mohawk Trail

FALL FOLIAGE ALONG THE TRAIL

This book covers an unusually scenic part of Western Massachusetts that was designated "The Mohawk Trail" at the dawn of the automobile age. It became the most popular auto trail in New England because of its relative remoteness, abundant water and spectacular fall foliage. Cool nights and sunny days create vivid colors in this region, which is more heavily treed today than it was in colonial times.

The core of the Mohawk Trail (that portion of Route 2 extending from the French King Bridge in Erving to Williamstown, near the New York border) is outdoor New England at its best, famous for its hiking trails, fishing, stunning bridges, river rafting and rolling countryside.

Our journey focuses on the most picturesque eastern two thirds of the Trail, extending from its beginnings outside Greenfield to Whitcomb Summit, the highest point. We summarize attractions and a special return route for those who want to continue on to North Adams. To capture some of the most scenic areas, we will venture off Route 2 into the surrounding hill towns.

Auto Trails

The arrival of the car in the late 19th and early 20th centuries led to the creation of "auto trails"– special routes given evocative names and marked with colored bands painted on utility poles. By the time that the United States implemented a numbered highways system in 1926, there were 48 major named auto trails.

On October 14, 1914, Route 2 was designated The Mohawk Trail with this red marker.

FALL FOLIAGE ALONG THE TRAIL

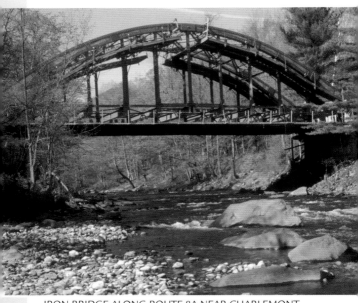

IRON BRIDGE ALONG ROUTE 8A NEAR CHARLEMONT

VINTAGE POSTCARD OF
MOHAWK TRAIL

The phrase "Mohawk Trail" conjures up visions of a narrow footpath made by local Indians. In fact, the current road only occasionally follows the early Indian path. Moreover, although parties of Mohawks hunted and fished this area, the Mohawks actually lived in what is now upstate New York. Under the leadership of Joseph Brandt (see insert), they sided with the British during the Revolutionary War and ultimately moved to Canada.

Thayendanegea, 1742–1807

JOSEPH BRANDT c. 1786, BY GILBERT STUART

A Mohawk Indian born in Ohio whom the historian Barbara Graymont calls "one of the most versatile and remarkable men in American history," Thayendanegea ("he places together two bets") became the principle chief of the Six Nations Indians. He fought for the British in the French and Indian Wars and remained a Loyalist during the U.S. War of Independence, during which he served with distinction as a British officer. In 1784, after the wars, he founded an Indian community on the Grand River in Ontario. A student of Latin and Greek, he helped translate Mark's Gospel into the Mohawk language. While he lived in European style at his house in Burlington, Ontario, he remained fiercely proud of his Indian ancestry, torn between two cultures.

But these are technicalities. "Trail" sounds more inviting than "road," and the Mohawks proved more marketable than local tribal candidates (Abanaki, Penobscott or the Pocumtucks, who lived along Deerfield River and in the middle Pioneer Valley).

During colonial times, the original Indian path was widened to accommodate wagon traffic and changed often to connect the communities that sprang up in these hills. In the late 18th century there was a toll road over parts of this "high country."

What turned this local road into a successful auto route was the creation of a wider, paved state highway across the Hoosac mountains.

Soon gift shops, tea rooms and "trading posts" sprang up. The Mohawk Trail became a popular destination with campgrounds and rustic cabins.

The trail emphasized its Indian heritage with giant statues of Indian chiefs, imitation teepees and colorful totem poles promoting the sale of "genuine" Indian artifacts.

TOTEM POLE ALONG
THE TRAIL

MOHAWK TRADING POST

28' HIGH BIG INDIAN

Erving

Our journey through this favored landscape begins on the border of Erving where the Millers River flows into the Connecticut River.

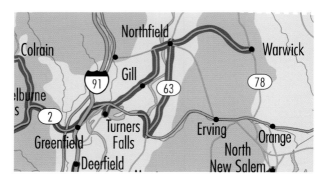

Here, in 1932, the state built the French King Bridge, a 750-foot, three-span, steel-decked arched bridge that connects Erving and Gill. A large rock in the center of the river was named the French King rock, in honor of King Louis XV of France, and the bridge was given the same name.

The top of the bridge provides a magnificent platform for viewing the foliage. Drive down the side access road (Dorsey Road) and observe the bridge from underneath. A dirt road and a bicycle path parallel the Connecticut River.

The center of Erving, the last town in Franklin County to be incorporated (1838), is about seven miles east of the bridge.

FRENCH KING BRIDGE

VIEW FROM FRENCH KING BRIDGE

The most colorful character to live in this part of Massachusetts was a Scottish actor, John Smith. In 1867 he moved into a cave in the hills above present-day Route 2. Visitors would hike up to what became known as "Erving Castle" and leave food and money, most of which the Hermit spent on caring for stray animals.

HERMIT'S CAVE SIGN

In 1868 George W. Barber published a pamphlet on Smith, entitled *The Hermit of Erving Castle*, and the hermit's fame spread. Articles periodically appeared in the *Athol Chronicle*, the *Turners Falls*

Reporter and the *Greenfield Gazette and Courier*. One account, published in 1874, claimed that 15,000 visitors had come to see him since his arrival.

Becoming too old to care for himself, John Smith was removed from Erving Castle on October 26, 1899, and sent to the Town Farm in Montague. He died about five months later and was buried in Erving Central Cemetery, along with his favorite cat, Toby. Not much is left of Erving Castle, but there is a well-marked trail up to the site.

JOHN SMITH AT
ERVING CASTLE

Northfield

In the 19th and 20th centuries the towns and villages near the French King Bridge were heavily industrialized, and today this stretch of Route 2 is not particularly picturesque. The most colorful building near the famous French King Bridge is the local bowling alley.

So rather than drive west along Route 2 toward Greenfield, we recommend navigating to Route 63 heading toward Northfield.

ALONG ROUTE 63 IN SPRING

Originally called Squakeag, Northfield enjoys fertile land that is spectacular in the spring, as fruit trees flower over beds of dandelions.

This wasn't always a peaceful area. Along with its neighbor Deerfield, Northfield suffered through decades of Indian attacks during the French and Indian Wars. Several monuments honor those who guarded this frontier community.

MONUMENT TO SETTLERS KILLED ON APRIL 15, 1747 (Courtesy of Northfield Historical Society)

MONUMENT TO CAPTAIN BEERS

As you enter Northfield along Route 63 you will notice a monument to Captain Richard Beers.

Beers and his men, who were delivering supplies, were killed in 1675 on the outskirts of Northfield during an Indian uprising referred to as King Philip's War. The actual site of the final fight was on a hill above and a little south of the marker.

FERRY CROSSING CONNECTICUT RIVER AT NORTHFIELD c. 1900
(Courtesy of Northfield Historical Society)

With the arrival of peace, Northfield, the most northern Massachusetts town in the fertile Pioneer Valley, flourished as an agricultural center.

In the 18th century, when steamships and barges plied a large stretch of the Connecticut River, Northfield was an important terminal.

Quinnetukut II, based in Northfield (800-859-2960), offers narrated tours of the Connecticut River.

There are still splendid old barns in Northfield, on the back-country roads.

As you drive into Northfield along Main Street, you are actually on the town common. Northfield has a linear common, a road bordered on both sides by grassy areas. The common is 165 feet wide. It begins at the intersection of Route 63 and Route 10 and extends for two miles.

NORTHFIELD TOBACCO BARN

WHITE HOUSE c. 1784 (Courtesy of Northfield Historical Society)

Elegant 18th- and 19th-century houses grace much of the common and other parts of Northfield. When the government documented historic American buildings during the Great Depression (a project that provided work for unemployed architects), over a dozen Northfield structures were included.

MAY DANCE AT SCHOOLHOUSE 1905 (Courtesy of Northfield Historical Society)

Northfield has an active Historical Society, headquartered in a former schoolhouse built in 1903-04.

The Northfield Historical Society has a comprehensive collection of photographs, paintings and other memorabilia.

FORMER NORTHFIELD SCHOOLHOUSE, NOW ON NATIONAL
REGISTER OF HISTORIC PLACES (Courtesy of Northfield
Historical Society)

The collection includes early 20th-century posters
used by Northfield merchants and an original Erastus
Salisbury Field portrait. Field was a traveling
portraitist whose work now hangs in many of the
country's best museums.

HISTORIC MERCHANT POSTERS

PORTRAIT OF CORNELIUS HILLIARD OF NORTHFIELD FARMS,
BY ERASTUS SALISBURY FIELD

Northfield is known to many as the site of the Northfield Mount Hermon School, formed by the merger of the two schools founded by the 19th-century evangelist, Dwight Lyman Moody.

Dwight L. Moody, 1837-1889

 A world-renowned evangelist and Christian leader, Moody was born in Northfield, Massachusetts, on February 5, 1837. He founded the Moody Bible Institute (America's oldest) and Moody Church in Chicago, the Northfield Seminary for Young Women (1879) and the Mount Hermon School for Young Men (1881). The two Northfield schools were combined in 1971 to form Northfield Mount Hermon, one of the country's leading college preparatory schools.

Moody funded the schools with proceeds from the sale of a hymn book that earned him $1.25 million in royalties, a huge sum in those days.

In 2005 Northfield Mount Hermon was consolidated on a single campus, which is located just south of Northfield, in the town of Gill. The original Northfield campus is for sale, with hopes to preserve its beauty and historic attractions.

The Northfield Center Cemetery, one of the earliest founded in Western Massachusetts, is also on the National Register of Historic Places. Probably the earliest contemporarily carved gravestone (1736) there is that of Stephen Belding.

GRAVESTONE OF STEPHEN BELDING, WHO DIED IN 1736

The gravestone reads (complete with mistakes):

HEAR LIETH
THE BODY OF MR
STEPHEN BELDING
WHO DIED FEBERUARY
THE 19: 1736 BEING
IN THE 47 YEAR OF
HIS AGE

The Center Cemetery is noted for images that are carved on many of the 18th-century grave markers. A number of the carvings were the work of Ebenezer James (1736-1808), a descendant of a first settler. The majority of the gravestones he carved are in the Northfield area and are much admired. A few of these unique gravestones, like that of Phinehas Wright, show an image of the deceased; others are "soul effigies," often angels.

GRAVESTONE OF COL. PHINEHAS WRIGHT OF NORTHFIELD

Phinehas Wright, a schoolmaster in Northfield, was chosen to be a representative and delegate to the Provincial Congress in 1774. He served as a colonel in the Revolutionary War, for which his grave, like that of all veterans, is honored with an American flag, placed there by the Veterans of Foreign Wars.

Perhaps the most treasured object in Northfield is the century-old Schell Memorial Bridge, which spans the Connecticut River. This architecturally rare beauty was completed in 1904 and survived the great flood of 1936. The bridge was closed in 1985 and has been slated for destruction for twenty years. The Friends of the Schell Bridge are working for its restoration. A picture of the bridge in 1904 is shown on the following pages, courtesy of Northfield Historical Society.

SCHELL MEMORIAL BRIDGE (FOLLOWING TWO PAGES)
(Courtesy of Northfield Historical Society)

Warwick

The next town on our itinerary is Warwick, a remote, hilly area popular with outdoor enthusiasts. Mt. Grace, the second-highest peak in Massachusetts, is located here. Warwick State Forest offers hiking, horseback riding,  cross-country skiing and snowmobiling. Sheomet Lake and the many area streams are popular fishing spots.

FISHING AT SHEOMET LAKE

DIRECTIONAL SIGNS, WARWICK VILLAGE

Warwick is seven miles east of Northfield. It can be reached via the Warwick – Northfield Road or as a separate trip from Route 2 via Route 78.

Warwick has a proud colonial history. The township was established by the Massachusetts General Court in 1736 to create a settlement that could help defend the Connecticut River Valley. The land was granted to the one survivor and the descendants of an expedition against the French in Canada, a raid that was led by Captain Andrew Gardner. In its early years the town was called Gardner's Canada.

WARWICK PUBLIC LIBRARY

It is not certain how the town got its name. The most likely explanation is that Warwick is named in honor of Guy, Earl of Warwick, who played a prominent role in the colonization of New England. Warwick is one of the oldest English earldoms.

Two millstones from the original grist mill sit in front of the Warwick Library, on the town common.

An iron fountain erected in 1900 serves the many bicycle riders who favor this hilly terrain.

IRON FOUNTAIN, WARWICK COMMON

ARTIST'S RENDITION OF WARWICK COMMON c. 1865
(Courtesy of Warwick Historical Society)

In the mid-1800s, Warwick was an industrial center, with sawmills, blacksmith shops, tanneries and factories turning out pails, staves and axes. The Nathan Jones Boot Shop, depicted as it was in 1865 in this contemporary painting, produced 20,000 pairs of boots each year, most of them sold to plantation owners in the South for their slaves. That business ended with the Civil War. Today the Town Hall sits on the site of the former boot shop.

The Warwick Historical Society, next door, is crammed with memorabilia, including a treasure trove of vintage images, like this late 19th-century photo of the oldest house in town.

WARWICK TOWN HALL

VINTAGE PHOTOGRAPH OF WARWICK'S OLDEST HOUSE
(Courtesy of Warwick Historical Society)

CIVIL WAR BATTLEFIELD
(courtesy Library of Congress)

The most moving artifact, though, is a rusted scythe with a notable history.

On a hot day in August 1862, the only son of Milton Bliss of Warwick left home to fight for the Union. The eighteen-year-old lad had been cutting briars in a field the day before his enlistment, and at workday's end he hung his scythe in the crotch of a young pine tree.

AUGUSTUS BLISS SCYTHE

Private Augustus Bliss of Company H, 36th Massachusetts Infantry, died shortly after the battle of Vicksburg. He is buried in an unmarked grave somewhere in the South.

Over the years the tree grew around Augustus Bliss's scythe, protected by a fence his father built in his son's memory. The scythe and part of the tree now occupy a place of honor at the Warwick Historical Society.

BELGIAN DRAFT HORSES

Warwick is typical of the small communities that are the heart of what is left of rural New England. Wandering the back roads can surprise and delight you. We found this team of Belgian draft horses leveling a private dirt road on the outskirts of Warwick.

While our team was photographing the young couple at the reins, an elderly lady stopped her car, walked over, and said, "I live in Warwick now, but I was raised in Maine seventy-six years ago, and this is exactly how my daddy leveled his roads."

ON TO
Gill

After returning to Northfield take Route 10 west. Don't miss the collection of old Autocar trucks sitting in a vacant field just outside of Northfield. First produced in 1907, the Autocar was the first four-cylinder engine, forward-control truck in the United States.

OLD AUTOCAR, ROUTE 10 OUTSIDE NORTHFIELD

MANY FARMS ARE FOUND ALONG BACK ROADS

If you stay on Route 10 you will reach the town of Bernardston, just north of Greenfield. Bernardston has some superb old homes and a famous mural depicting the hoe factory that was located there in the 19th century.

You don't want to miss Gill. The Gill–Turners Falls Road (just off Route 10) will take you through some wonderful farmland directly to our next destination.

HOE FACTORY MURAL, BERNARDSTON

MEMORIAL CHAPEL

Along the way you will pass the consolidated campus of Northfield Mount Hermon.

The Mount Hermon campus has an all-weather, 400-meter track and 27 playing fields.

MOUNT HERMON SIGN

MOUNT HERMON TRACK

COUNTRY BARN IN A FIELD OF CORN

The back-country roads of Gill are dotted with streams and rolling pastures.

Charming old barns are nestled in fields of corn.

HORSE IN A GILL FIELD

STREAM IN GILL

FALLS AT GILL, 1818 BY ORRA WHITE HITCHCOCK
(Courtesy of Amherst College)

Gill was formerly part of Deerfield. It was incorporated in 1793, named to honor then-Lieutenant Governor Moses Gill.

The Connecticut River meanders through the entire length of the town.

The largest and most magnificent falls along the Connecticut River were at the southern edge of Gill, on the Gill–Montague border. The Native Americans fished for shad and salmon here at the place they called Peskeompskut, which means "split rock at the falls." This was the scene of one of the bloodiest battles during King Philip's War.

On the evening of May 18, 1767, an English force under the command of Captain William Turner of Hadley surprised a large band of Wampaneog Indians camped near the falls, killing several hundred. Turner was mortally wounded during an Indian counter-attack.

Unfortunately, the falls along the river were an impediment to navigation and in later times they fell victim to a rapidly industrializing Massachusetts.

The great falls at Gill became the site of the first dam built on the Connecticut River. An entrepreneur, Alvah Crocker, created the mill town of Turners Falls here in the 1870s, selling industrial sites to manufacturers and home sites to hundreds of skilled immigrants from French Canada, Ireland, Germany, Poland and Lithuania who were attracted to the booming area.

MONTAGUE BRIDGE IN GILL, LEADING TO VILLAGE OF TURNERS FALLS

Turners Falls

GREAT FALLS DISCOVERY CENTER

A visit to Turners Falls is now a must stop on any journey in this region. In October 2003 the Great Falls Discovery Center opened.

INTERIOR DISPLAY
(Courtesy of Discovery Center)

GREAT HALL

This is a fascinating educational complex that tells the story of the Connecticut River. There are superb displays of the local habitat, models of the Connecticut River watershed and tanks that hold native fish.

An elegant brick building known as the Great Hall is available for meetings. This was originally a machine shop for the paper company that occupied the site. Montague Paper was the largest supplier of newsprint in the United States in the early decades of the 20th century. Water from the nearby canal supplied horsepower for heating, steaming and drying the newsprint.

Great Falls Discovery Center

Avenue A, Turners Falls, MA 01376

Hours: 10:00 a.m. to 4:00 p.m. Fridays and Saturdays, except holidays

Telephone: 413-545-5353 (Discovery Center) or 413-663-0209 (Silvio O. Conte National Fish and Wildlife Refuge)

A comprehensive website on the Conte Refuge is available at www.fws.gov/r5soc/main.htm

Further information available at www.mass.gov/dcr

POWER CANAL, TURNERS FALLS

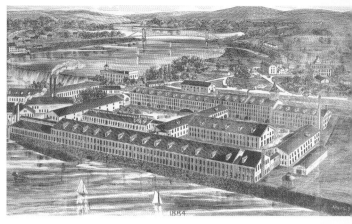

JOHN RUSSELL CUTLERY CO, 1884
GREENFIELD GAZETTE CENTENNIAL EDITION

The old power canal created by Alvah Crocker is located just behind the Discovery Center.

Turners Falls was a major center of industry in the 19th century.

In addition to several paper companies, cheap land and ample water power attracted the John Russell Cutlery Company to Turners Falls in 1870. The huge Russell works soon employed over 650 workers and used 700 tons of steel a year. Output included over 150 variations of pocket knives, a product previously imported into the United States. The famous Bowie knife was also manufactured at this site.

The mills are silent now. Luckily a few buildings have been converted to other uses. The water still flows swiftly though the canal, which is fenced in and posted.

SIGN POSTED ALONG CANAL

Just across the street from the Discovery Center, on Avenue A, is the venerable Shady Glen Diner, which has ably served the community for almost fifty years. Any eatery that serves fresh corn on the cob in season deserves to be a tourist attraction.

SHADY GLEN DINER

SPRING ALONG THE CONNECTICUT RIVER

Turners Falls has a large number of splendid churches reflecting its rich ethnic heritage. The steeple of St. Mary's Roman Catholic Church, completed in 1888, is a prominent landmark.

Our Lady of Czestochowa attracts visitors from everywhere. The church contains an important copy of a centuries old painting, *Our Lady of Jasna Gora* (which means "bright hill"). The original is in Czestochowa, Poland.

ST. MARYS CHURCH, 1888
FROM GREENFIELD GAZETTE
CENTENNIAL EDITION

OUR LADY OF JASNA GORA
(Courtesy of Our Lady of
  Czestochowa)

Greenfield

WELCOME TO
GREENFIELD

The town of Greenfield is situated at the confluence of the Green and Connecticut Rivers. You reach Greenfield by taking Route 2A from the center of Turners Falls or exiting Interstate 91 at the Greenfield rotary and following Route 2A into the center.

The main street is a busy thoroughfare of local shops. Travel writer Christina Tree extols Greenfield for still "having all the downtown essentials that most towns used to have but have lost since the 1950s."

DOWNTOWN GREENFIELD

GREENFIELD TOWN HALL

Greenfield was originally part of Deerfield but was incorporated in 1753 as a separate town. It was selected as the seat of Franklin County in 1811. Greenfield became a major manufacturing center in the late 19th century. A large community college was established in Greenfield in 1960. As a result of all these factors, Greenfield is now a sizable, modern city.

A large mural, just off Main Street, celebrates the town's rich past.

GREENFIELD MURAL

PUMPING STATION COVERED BRIDGE, GREENFIELD

EARLY PHOTOGRAPH OF 1870 COVERED BRIDGE FROM
GREENFIELD GAZETTE CENTENNIAL EDITION

Greenfield has an historic covered bridge. The Pumping Station Bridge was built over the Green River in 1870.

The original bridge was destroyed in a Halloween fire in 1969. Thanks largely to private donations, the structure was quickly rebuilt and is now closed to vehicles.

A sign near the bridge marks the spot where Eunice Williams, the wife of Deerfield's pastor, was killed in 1704. Captured in the raid on Deerfield during the French and Indian Wars, she did not have the strength for the 300-mile march to Canada.

WOODEN TRAIN

Greenfield recently created a 1.25-acre community greenspace in the heart of downtown, called Energy Park. The wooden play train is a favorite of children.

This child-friendly park is located at the site of the town train station, which operated from 1881 to 1963. It contains a replica of the train depot, an authentic 1944 caboose, the play train, public art and several fascinating educational displays about sustainable energy.

The park has became a gathering place for concerts and community events, and is a perfect spot for lunch.

The Chamber of Commerce (on Main Street across from the library) and the Visitors Center (at 18 Miner Street, just off Route 2; 413-773-9393) are useful sources of information on the entire area.

The Greenfield Public Library was designed by Asher Benjamin, a seminal figure in the architecture of New England.

DOWNTOWN "STATION DISPLAY"

GREENFIELD LIBRARY

Greenfield's most famous landmark is Poet's Seat Tower, set on a high bluff overlooking the town.

Because of the site's commanding view, a wooden tower was erected here in the 1870s. It burned to the ground in 1908.

In 1912 a stone tower was erected on this site, with a plaque honoring a noted Greenfield poet.

Poet's Seat Tower offers a splendid view of Greenfield.

Greenfield, located at the intersection of Interstate 91 and Route 2, is a natural entry point to the Mohawk Trail region. Its historic attractions and abundant resources lead many visitors to make it their base.

POET'S SEAT TOWER

EARLY TOWER (Author's Collection)

VIEW FROM POET'S SEAT TOWER

ON TO
Colrain

As you continue on climbing up the Trail you will see Old Greenfield Village on the left. This tourist attraction is a cluster of buildings that display New England life circa 1895. This private collection of hundreds of artifacts 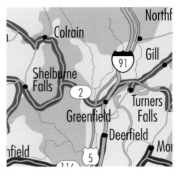 was assembled by a retired school teacher, Wayne Morse. it's open weekends from May through October.

There are streams, lakes and rivers to enjoy throughout the Mohawk Trail region, which is noted for its fishing.

DISPLAY AT OLD GREENFIELD VILLAGE

FISHING THE DEERFIELD RIVER

Fields of flowers have become the backdrop for abandoned farm tools from an earlier era.

OLD PLOW IN A FIELD OF FLOWERS

COLRAIN APPLES

This is serious apple country, particularly on the roads branching off the Trail to the north.

If you stay on the Mohawk Trail all the way to the intersection with Route 112 (about eight miles), you will pass Gould's Sugar House, a popular destination during maple-sugaring season (March and April). Gould's opens again in the fall (September and October; 413-625-6170).

GOULD'S SUGAR HOUSE

FIRST CONGREGATIONAL CHURCH OF SHELBURNE

The First Congregational Church of Shelburne, established in 1770, sits on a hill above the Trail. Because of its commanding location and appearance, this is one of the most photographed churches in Massachusetts.

Colrain, one of the more picturesque towns in the entire Mohawk Trail region, lies to the north of the Trail. It can be reached on Route 112 or by taking the Colrain – Shelburne Road on the outskirts of Shelburne.

VIEW OF BRICK MEETING
HOUSE COMING INTO TOWN

The Colrain – Shelburne Road climbs into the hills and weaves through apple orchards and farmland, then descends steeply into Colrain's town center, offering a view of the Brick Meeting House.

The town was settled in the colonial era and incorporated in 1761. It is thought to have been named after Lord Colraine, an Irish Peer. Many of the town's early settlers came from Northern Ireland and Scotland.

PICTURESQUE COLRAIN

COLRAIN "CITY" LOOKING SOUTH 1892
GREENFIELD GAZETTE CENTENNIAL EDITION

Colrain could be mistaken for rural Vermont, the state
it borders.

Nestled among heavily treed hills, Colrain offers a
captivating view from all of the three roads that
connect at the town center.

The meeting house (the original Congregational
Church) is now used for special events.

BRICK MEETING HOUSE

Colrain's citizens are justly proud of the fact that a town schoolhouse on Catamount Hill (in the southwest part of Colrain) was the first public school in the United States to fly the American flag. During the War of 1812, one Amasa Shippee, a loyalist who had just enlisted for service,

1810 SCHOOLHOUSE

conceived the idea of showing support for the war by erecting a flag over the schoolhouse, which was the center of social and educational life. The raising of the flag, in May 1812, was a grand occasion.

Although the one-room Catamount Hill school no longer exists, one of the oldest (1810) red brick schools in the country is in Colrain, on Shelburne Line Road.

In 1800, Colrain, with a population of 2,014, was the largest of the towns in what would become Franklin County. The early decades of the 19th century were prosperous. Colrain's ample water, from two branches of the North River, attracted cotton and woolen mills, an iron foundry and much light manufacturing. Colrain was also known for its large herds of sheep.

The town's most prominent icon, shown on the sign coming into town, was the picturesque Arthur A. Smith Covered Bridge in the Lyonsville section of Colrain.

WELCOME TO OLD COLERAINE

In the 1870s Colrain had eleven covered bridges. By 1951 the last surviving bridge was the Arthur A. Smith Bridge, spanning the North River. The original bridge on this spot, built in 1870, was a long plank bridge that was not covered. Late one afternoon in 1895, Arthur Smith's hired hand, who had been instructed to drive the cows across the bridge one by one, lost control of the herd. As the local paper reported, "[the cows] rushed over in a mad scramble. There was an ominous cracking of timber and the bridge broke in the middle as the cows fell into the river." There is no record of how many cows survived, but the bridge was a total loss. In 1896 the town moved an abandoned covered bridge, the Fox Bridge, to this spot. This 99-foot beauty carried traffic for almost a century until it was removed from its mooring in 1991. What remains now rests forlornly in a field off Route 112.

REMAINS OF ARTHUR A. SMITH COVERED BRIDGE

Massachusetts has only six authentic 19th-century covered bridges left, and several of these are waiting for reconstruction. The state is slowly restoring these precious structures, typically rebuilding them from scratch using the original design. If ever a town deserved a restored covered bridge, it is Colrain.

Coming into town from nearby Vermont on Route 112 offers a splendid view of the steeple of the church, framed against the encircling hills.

The Colrain Historical Society is located on Main Street in the former house of G. William Pitt, a noted musician and patron of the arts. The building contains Pitt's antiques, artwork and theater memorabilia, as well as other town artifacts.

This is an area in which to wander the back roads.

APPROACHING COLRAIN TOWN CENTER ON ROUTE 112 FROM VERMONT

SUGAR SHACK AND COWS

SPRING VISTA

MINIATURE SICILIAN DONKEY

You will find picturesque barns, sugarhouses and a cider mill, fields full of flowers and crops, and all forms of livestock, including, if you are lucky, a miniature Sicilian donkey.

WOODSLAWN FARM IN COLRAIN

Colrain still has working farms along its charming back-country roads. Recently, the Woodslawn Farm in Colrain was designated a National Bicentennial Farm, meaning it has been in the same family for over 200 years.

COWS IN FRONT OF THE BROWN HOMESTEAD FARM

THE PURINGTON FARM IN AUTUMN

Patric duBreuil, a local photographer, has captured the essence of rural Colrain in several awesome panoramic photographs. A portion of his photograph of the Brown Homestead Farm appears below.

The heavily treed, hilly countryside around Colrain bursts into color in the fall. Those who seek a less congested way to see the fall foliage would be smart to visit Colrain in early October.

We continue our journey by driving south on Route 112, which will take you to the center of Shelburne Falls.

Be sure to stop and look at the old John Deere tractor on the outskirts of Shelburne.

EARLY DEERE TRACTOR

Shelburne Falls

Shelburne Falls, just off Route 2, has become a vibrant center of the entire Mohawk Trail corridor. This is not a town but a Victorian era village comprised of the commercial centers of Shelburne and Buckland.

The Shelburne Falls Village Information Center (413-625-2544), headquartered in a former fire station at 75 Bridge Street, has useful handout material and pleasant volunteers.

SHELBURNE FALLS CENTER

ENJOYING A SUNNY DAY IN SHELBURNE FALLS

There are plenty of places to eat and shop in Shelburne Falls. There are also classic American buildings like the VFW Hall along the bustling side streets.

The town of Shelburne was first settled in 1712, when the area was part of Deerfield. It was incorporated in 1768 and named for Lord Shelburne of England. The first Yale locks were made in Shelburne by Linus Yale, who was born here in 1851.

VFW HALL

FLOWERS ALONG THE BRIDGE

1908 TROLLEY BRIDGE, NOW THE BRIDGE OF FLOWERS

BRIDGE OF FLOWERS SIGN

The most famous attraction, though, is what has come to be called the Bridge of Flowers.

In 1919 the local garden clubs began planting flowers along an active trolley bridge, as a World War I memorial. After trolley service was discontinued in 1926, the entire bridge was planted with flowers.

Now over 500 species of flowers are in bloom from spring through fall. The Bridge of Flowers is meticulously maintained by the Shelburne Falls Women's Club. The pedestrians-only bridge offers splendid views of the Deerfield River.

FLAG FLYING ON THE BRIDGE OF FLOWERS

VIEW FROM BRIDGE OVER DEERFIELD RIVER

Shelburne Falls in recent years has become a significant arts and crafts center, offering everything from handmade leather goods and jewelry to world-class quilts and blown glass.

A SCENE AT NORTH RIVER GLASS

Shelburne Falls is also the site of dramatic glacial potholes and a great falls where there was once superb salmon fishing.

The Mohawk and Penobscott Indians, who were often at war, signed a fishing treaty in 1708 that preserved this site for all tribes, a pact that was later recognized by the Colonial Court.

There is a hydroelectric dam along the river now, but the water still flows rapidly past the rocks that contain some fifty potholes created after the last glaciers receded, about 13,000 years ago.

These glacial potholes range in size from 6 inches to 39 feet across.

SALMON FALLS SIGN

Salmon Falls and the glacial potholes can be viewed from an observation deck at the end of Deerfield Street. Access to the river is now restricted, and special arrangements have to be made to view the potholes up close.

STROLLING ALONG THE BRIDGE

VIEW OF GLACIAL POTHOLES FROM BUCKLAND

WHEN ACCESS WAS PERMITTED

Buckland

Be sure to visit the "other" side of the Deerfield River. An 1890 iron bridge connects the Shelburne and Buckland sides of Shelburne Falls.

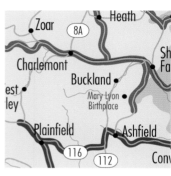

Don't drive over the bridge. Cross on foot in order to take in the view and enjoy a "soothing, relaxing massage" at the shop perched at the edge of the river.

1890 IRON BRIDGE CONNECTING BUCKLAND AND SHELBURNE

As you pass into Buckland, note the former Odd Fellows Hall, built in 1877. It now houses McCusker's Market and Deli, which specializes in natural foods.

MCCUSKER'S MARKET

MASSAGES, ANYONE?

TROLLEY #10 (Courtesy of Shelburne Falls Trolley Museum)

TROLLEY YARD

SHELBURNE FALLS TROLLEY
MUSEUM RUINS

Like most towns at the turn of the 20th century, Buckland and Shelburne had trolley service. When the trolleys were discontinued in 1926, a local farmer, Marshall Johnson, acquired the last trolley car. The Johnson family used the old trolley as a chicken coop for sixty-five years.

Trolley #10 was restored to its former glory by enthusiastic volunteers in 1996 and now serves as the main attraction at the Shelburne Falls Trolley Museum (which is actually in Buckland).

On weekends you can ride the trolley around the local train yard while a volunteer conductor describes the

sights that you would have encountered during the seven-mile run between Shelburne Falls and Colrain.

The trolley museum contains a visitor's center with a great collection of model trains. The ruins of old trolley cars sit atop what was the foundation of a large shed, where milk and cream and other goods were stored.

FOUNDATION OF MARY LYON'S BIRTHPLACE

Buckland is another interesting area in which to explore back-country roads.

The old Baptist Corner Cemetery is on Bray Road, a few miles past the trolley museum.

The birthplace of Mary Lyon, who founded Mount Holyoke College, is about nine miles up a winding country road (near the end, a dirt road) high above the town of Buckland.

Mt. Holyoke College maintains the site as a memorial.

Mary Lyon, 1797-1849

Mary Lyon was born on February 28, 1797, in Buckland, Massachusetts. She was the founder of Mount Holyoke Female Seminary (now Mount Holyoke College) and a pioneer in women's education. In 1987 she was honored with a U.S. postage stamp.

Visitors to Shelburne Falls assume that they have seen Buckland if they crossed over the bridge to the commercial section of the town. However, the original town center is about two miles away, on Old Upper Road, off Route 112. Route 112 is also the most direct way to reach the Lyon homestead.

The 1785 Congregational Church and the Buckland Historical Museum are located in the old town center.

Buckland was formed from a plantation in Charlemont with the unpromising name of "No-Town." The town was incorporated in 1779.

The Buckland Historical Museum is located in the former town schoolhouse. It has a good collection of Civil War relics, early tools, needlework and other memorabilia.

BUCKLAND HISTORICAL MUSEUM

ON TO
Charlemont

The Mohawk Trail between Shelburne Falls and Charlemont is picturesque and full of vintage Americana.

The Indian Plaza Gift Shop and Pow Wow grounds (413-339-4096) is the one location along the Trail where, between May and early October, Native American tribes hold periodic pow wows.

The Big Indian Shop (413-625-6817) is a classic souvenir shop that has been in the same family since the 1930s. This must stop for kids has live animals, a tepee and a 28-foot-tall wooden Indian.

BIG INDIAN SHOP

POW WOW DANCER

1828 BRICK SCHOOLHOUSE

MARANATHA BAPTIST CHURCH

COVERED BRIDGE ANTIQUES COMPLEX

There are motels, an antiques complex and an historic 1828 brick schoolhouse along this stretch of road. The simple Maranatha Baptist Chapel, with a cemetery next to it, is still in active use.

Charlemont is located along a fertile flood plain first settled in the mid-1700s. The original name, Chickley's Town, was changed to Charley's Mount, which was soon simplified to Charlemont.

FEDERATED CHURCH

The acoustically perfect Federated Church (413-625-9511) in the center of Charlemont is the venue for Mohawk Trail Concerts, which draw audiences from all over New England. Tickets can be ordered at www.mohawktrailconcerts.org.

The Charlemont Inn (413-339-5796), also in the town center, dates back to 1787. It is a legitimate historic site as well as a functioning business offering a dozen rooms and full meal service throughout the year. The inn also serves as a turkey-checking station in the spring.

Wild turkeys were so successfully restored to their Western Massachusetts habitat by MassWildlife in the 1970s that there are now spring and fall gobbler-hunting seasons.

Turkey hunting requires a high degree of skill; fewer than one in fifteen hunters succeeds in bagging one of these prized game birds.

CHARLEMONT INN

SUCCESSFUL TURKEY HUNTER

The Main Street Café and Country Store is at the junction of Routes 2 and 8A in Charlemont.

Take 8A north, past the café and its home delivery fleet, to reach the Bissell Covered Bridge, which is now open only to pedestrians.

DELIVERY WAGON PARKED BEHIND CAFÉ

Windows along the side of the bridge let you look at the water tumbling underneath as you walk through.

MILL BROOK WATERFALL

TWO VIEWS OF BISSELL COVERED BRIDGE

Heath

Route 8A north past the Bissell Bridge will bring you to the hill town of Heath. You can also reach Heath from the Mohawk Trail on Avery Brook Road, which will take you to the Town Center.

Heath is a classic hill town. It has a large common (laid out in 1706) surrounded by white clapboard buildings.

Heath was incorporated as a separate town in 1785. Former Supreme Court Justice Felix Frankfurter spent summers here.

HEATH COMMON

HISTORICAL MARKER ON THE COMMON WITH OLD TOWN
HOUSE IN DISTANCE

The Union Church, on the edge of the common, is
still in active use.

The Heath Historical
Society maintains three
historic buildings in town:
the original schoolhouse,
the Old Town House
(where town meetings
were held) and the
Solomon Temple Barn.

HEATH UNION CHURCH

Fort Shirley

To protect the growing settlements in the Pioneer Valley against Indian attack, a line of forts was constructed on the hills overlooking the Valley in the 1740s. One of the most important installations was Fort Shirley, built in 1744 in the northeast part of present-day Heath.

The fort was commanded by the newly commissioned Captain Ephraim Williams, Jr., who later went on to command Fort Massachusetts and played an important role in the founding of Williamstown.

PAINTING OF MARTHA GALE SPOONER

The Society's extensive collection includes drawings, vintage photos and oil paintings of 19th-century inhabitants of Heath, like Martha Gale Spooner, who died at the age of 98 in 1874.

Among the most interesting objects in the Heath Historical Society buildings are samples of the straw hats hand-woven there in the early 19th century.

STRAW HATS IN HEATH HISTORICAL SOCIETY COLLECTION

THE EMERSON FAMILY OF HEATH 1836

The women of Heath, like those in many of the towns in Western Massachusetts supplemented their income in the winter months by weaving straw hats.

A middleman brought palm leaves up from the Carolinas. The women would then bleach the leaves, split them in two and braid them. This was big business. About 30,000 hats were made in Heath in 1837.

The oil painting of the Dr. Joseph Emerson family in the Old Town House is a folk art masterpiece that has been widely exhibited at museums in New England. Dr. Emerson was the town's doctor for thirty-six years in the early decades of the 19th century.

KINSMAN GRAVESTONE

A little north of the town common (take Bray Road) is the old Center Cemetery. The cemetery contains the graves of early settlers like Samuel Kinsman, who came to Heath in 1792 as an ambitious 23-year-old and developed one of the area's major farms.

The gravestones here are a moving testimony to the harsh life that often claimed women early — women like Samuel's first wife Kezia, who died at age thirty-six.

Just across from the cemetery is a large field where the Heath Agricultural Society Fair is held two weekends before Labor Day each year, offering genuine horse

THE CENTER CEMETERY

SOLOMON TEMPLE BARN

and oxen draws, games, and plenty of food. A square dance and fireworks are prime attractions. Every year there is a new design for the Heath Fair T-shirt, which have become collectables.

At the back of this field is the Solomon Temple barn, one of the oldest barns in Western Massachusetts, which

now houses a superb collection of farm implements, wagons and other historic displays. This structure is managed by the Heath Historic Society.

When you're done exploring Heath, return to the Mohawk Trail heading west.

SITE OF HEATH FAIR

ON TO THE
Summit

After you pass through the center of Charlemont, the Deerfield River widens. Swimming and rafting trips are quite popular along this stretch of the Trail. Three water adventure companies are eager to provide everything from family float trips to Class IV whitewater trips on the upper reaches of the Deerfield River, below Monroe Bridge.

ZOAR OUTDOORS, ALONG ROUTE 2

GATHERING FOR WHITEWATER SPORTS INSTRUCTION

Whitewater Trips

Zoar Outdoors
800-532-7482 • www.zoaroutdoor.com

The area's oldest rafting company. Has a guest lodge and campground.

Crab Apple Whitewater
800-553-7238 • www.crabappleinc.com/index.shtml

This Maine-based company with a local facility along the Deerfield River has been offering rafting or inflatable kayaking in Massachusetts for over a decade.

Moxie Outdoor Adventures
800-866-6943 • www.moxierafting.com

Offers trips on the Deerfield River and several rivers in Maine.

WADING IN THE RIVER

HAIL TO THE SUNRISE STATUE

WISHING POOL

There was a toll bridge over the river here in the late 18th century. Travelers often forded the river rather than pay the toll. A "Shunpike" marker honors these pioneers whose thriftiness led to free travel on all Massachusetts roads starting in 1810.

Mohawk Park, on the outskirts of Charlemont, is the center point of the Mohawk Trail. Here in 1932 the Improved Order of Red Men erected a bronze statue whose tablet reads "Hail to the Sunrise – in Memory of the Mohawk Indian."

A wishing pool commemorates scores of native tribes throughout the United States.

The western half of the Trail is sparsely populated, and much of the land is state forests.

MOHAWK TRAIL STATE FOREST

ROLLING HILLS ALONG THE TRAIL

Driving along this stretch of Route 2 offers endless vistas of rolling hills, beautiful any time of year, spectacular during the peak foliage season.

As you climb up the Hoosac mountain range, you will reach the curiously named town of Florida, which was first settled in 1783. Florida is about ten miles from Charlemont.

There are two theories about the name: that is was chosen out of defiance (Florida is said to be the coldest spot in the state) or that it was simply a name in the news early in the 19th century. Since the town was incorporated in 1805, fourteen years before the acquisition of the state of Florida from Spain, we favor the defiance theory.

WELCOME TO FLORIDA

EASTERN PORTAL OF THE
HOOSAC TUNNEL

The town of Florida has a fascinating history. It was a boom town in the second half of the 19th century when it was the base camp for a 24-year project to

AN INSIDE VIEW OF THE HOOSAC
TUNNEL c. 1875 (Author's Collection)

dig a massive tunnel through Hoosac Mountain, to complete the rail link between Boston and the west. One hundred ninety-five men lost their lives digging the four-mile-long tunnel before the job was finished in 1875.

WHITEWATER RAFTING ON THE DEERFIELD

The adventurous can drive down a very steep Whitcomb Hill Road (part of the old trail over the Hoosac Mountains) to see the eastern portal of the Hoosac Tunnel. There is a parking lot where you can watch a train going through the tunnel, if you are lucky.

A better reason for making this side journey is that at the base of Whitcomb Hill, River Road parallels the Deerfield River for miles. Following River Road north, you are likely to see kayakers and rafters speed by.

You are virtually certain to see anglers fishing what is considered one of the best trout streams in the country. The Deerfield River widens to as much as 150 feet a couple miles beyond the Eastern Portal. This entire area

EASTERN SUMMIT

VIEWING AT WHITCOMB SUMMIT

ELK MEMORIAL AT WHITCOMB SUMMIT

is a paradise for hikers, birders and all those who love to fish.

There are three vantage points along the high points of the Trail. The first viewing platform is at the Eastern Summit, which has a gift shop open during the summer and fall.

Whitcomb Summit itself (a little over a mile past Eastern Summit) is the highest point along the Trail. It has a motel (open mid-May to mid-November), eight vintage cabins and a "hundred-mile view."

A magnificent bronze statue of an elk was erected at the summit in 1923 as a memorial to members of the Benevolent and Protective Order of Elks (BPOE) who lost their lives in WWI.

A short distance further along the Trail, the Western Summit offers a grand view of the northern Berkshires. The Wigwam Cottages, perched at the edge of the summit, have been taking in guests since the 1920s.

WIGWAM CABINS

FALL FOLIAGE ALONG THE TRAIL

North Adams
AND WILLIAMSTOWN

When you continue on the Trail past Western Summit heading toward North Adams (about nine miles away), you are in the northern part of the region known popularly as "The Berkshires." This culturally blessed part of Massachusetts deserves days of exploration, and even then you will only begin to appreciate its riches.

Some travelers who are pressed for time end their tour of the Mohawk Trail at Whitcomb Summit. Others turn around there in order to revisit Shelburne Falls or return to Charlemont for a concert at the Federated Church.

However, if you do drive further along the Trail, take your time navigating the Hairpin Turn.

This was a must stop in the 1920s, as the vintage postcard shows. Early model cars had difficulty navigating the turn.

Once you manage the turn and head down the final steep slope, you will soon be in the former mill town of North Adams.

HAIRPIN TURN AHEAD

EARLY POSTCARD OF HAIRPIN TURN

With a population of about 15,000, this is the largest town in the Northern Berkshires. Located at the confluence of the two branches of the Hoosac River, North Adams was a center of manufacturing for 200 years. The armor plates for the Civil War ironclad *USS Monitor* were forged here.

LITHOGRAPH DEPICTING THE EPIC 1862 BATTLE OF THE *MONITOR* AND THE *MERRIMAC* (Courtesy of Library of Congress)

4In 1999 the former industrial space vacated by Sprague Electric (the last major manufacturer in the town) was converted into a massive center for contemporary visual and performing arts. The Massachusetts Museum of Contemporary Art, or MASS MoCA, is the largest contemporary art center in the United States. It has nineteen galleries and over 100,000 square feet of exhibit space, along with theaters and courtyards where performances are held.

North Adams has been the focus of considerable urban renewal in recent years. The Western Gateway State Park at 115 State Street, in the freightyard district (open daily from 10:00 a.m. to 5:00 p.m. year round), contains an extensive display on the construction of the Hoosac Tunnel and the area's rich railroad history. The park is also home to the North Adams Museum of History & Science (open Thursday – Sunday, 10:00 a.m. to 5:00 p.m.), whose 25 exhibits tell the story of the Northern Berkshires.

MASS MoCA

1040 Mass MoCA Way, North Adams, MA 01247
Hours: 11:00 a.m. – 5:00 p.m. daily (longer in summer)
413-662-2111 • www.massmoca.org

MASS MOCA

MOUNT GREYLOCK

Those who favor the outdoors should explore Mount
Greylock, the highest peak (3,491 feet) in
Massachusetts. Follow the well-marked road through
Mount Greylo.ck State Reservation, beginning just
outside North Adams and exiting onto Route 7, south
of Ashley Falls. The park is open between 9:00 a.m.
and 5:00 p.m. from Memorial Day to Columbus Day.

The cultural center of the Northern Berkshires is
Williamstown, five miles west of North Adams. The area,
settled in 1753, was initially know as Hoosuck Plantation.
It was renamed Williamstown to honor Colonel Ephraim
Williams (1716-1755), who, in 1744, erected the area's
first military outpost, known as Fort Massachusetts. Col.
Williams was killed in the Battle of Lake George. His will
bequeathed money to maintain a school in the
community, provided the town change its name.

WILLIAMS COLLEGE

That school became Williams College, whose handsome buildings mingle with private homes in what is called "The Village Beautiful." Located at the confluence of the Green and Hoosic Rivers, Williamstown is a gem.

The Northern Berkshires are renowned for their art museums. In addition to MASS MoCA, the Williams College Museum of Art (www.williams.edu/WMCA, 413-597-2429) is one of the finest college art museums in the country. The Sterling and Francine Clark Art Institute in Williamstown attracts art lovers from all over the world for the outstanding collection of French Impressionist paintings that Clark and his French wife,

CLARK ART INSTITUTE (Photograph by Darlene Bordwell)

Francine, began to assemble in 1916. The museum also has an extensive number of 19th-century American paintings and early photographs. The museum's core building is a white marble neoclassic structure built in 1955.

Sterling and Francine Clark Art Institute

225 South Street, Williamstown, MA 01267
Hours: 10:00 a.m.– 5:00 p.m. Tues.– Sun
(daily in July and August)
413-458-2303 • www.clarkart.edu

If your travel plans permit, stay over at least one night in North Adams or Williamstown in order to begin to explore the area's riches. Even a one-or two -day visit will be a special capstone to your tour of the Mohawk Trail.

Consider returning to your ultimate destination by taking Route 7 south, rather than retracing the entire Mohawk Trail. Route 2 connects with Route 7 outside Williamstown. From this intersection you are about 30 miles from an entrance to Interstate 90 (the "Mass Pike"). This hour-long trip will take you through the heart of the northern and central Berkshires.

FIRST CONGREGATIONAL CHURCH OF WILLIAMSTOWN

Final Thoughts

Many people associate the Mohawk Trail region with the peak fall foliage season, of course, but its real appeal is much more broad.

FALL SCENE

The spring is an invigorating time to visit, as daffodils, hyacinth and tulips begin to emerge on the Bridge of Flowers and throughout the area.

The spring and summer are perfect for hiking and biking and the many water sports for which the area is famous. Hot-air ballooning is popular much of the year.

In early September the Franklin County Fair offers a special treat. This is one of the oldest fairs in the country, first staged in 1848.

In the winter months, cross-country skiing is popular throughout the region.

HOT-AIR BALLOONING
OUTSIDE OF GREENFIELD

FRANKLIN COUNTY FAIR

Properly enjoying this part of Massachusetts takes effective planning. The next sections of this guide offer a broad range of choices on where to stay, a particularly critical decision for a journey that extends over 60 miles. We also offer a vast number of resources to aid you in your planning.

Enjoy!

ENJOYING THE SNOW

ACCOMMODATIONS

The Mohawk Trail region is a great choice for a long weekend or vacation. However, because of the distances involved in visiting the area's many interesting sites and the area's touring legacy, you should plan where to stay with some care. Be sure to make reservations, particularly at the height of the foliage season.

Those who prefer to stay "right along the Trail" will find a number of of motels that extend from the French King Bridge to North Adams. There are also bed & breakfast accommodations in most of the towns covered in this journey, including the hill towns. Some of these facilities are seasonal and their status can change. The best source for current motel and B&B information is the Visitors Center in Greenfield, which publishes a Lodging Guide twice a year (413-773-9393).

For a special experience, consider staying at an area inn or a hotel at the end of the Trail, in the Berkshires. Here are four excellent choices:

Charlemont Inn, a venerable 1787 inn that has served Mohawk Trail visitors for over 215 years

Main Street
Charlemont
413-339-5796
www.charlemontinn.com

14 rooms and 2 suites
Full meal service

Deerfield Inn, a classic country inn built in 1884, located in the historic town of Deerfield, just south of Greenfield

81 Old Main Street
Deerfield, MA 01342-0305
413-774-5587
800-926-3865
www.deerfieldinn.com

23 rooms
Full service

The Porches Inn, a new facility located in six renovated Victorian era row houses near Mass MoCA in North Adams

231 River Street
North Adams, MA 01247
413-664-0400
www.porches.com

52 rooms
Breakfast
Internet access

Orchards Hotel, a small elegant hotel with a charming interior courtyard, on the eastern edge of Williamstown

222 Adams Road
Williamstown, MA 01267
www.orchardshotel.com

45 rooms, 2 suites
Full meal service

SUPPLEMENTAL READING

The Berkshire Hills & Pioneer Valley of Western Massachusetts, by Christina Tree & William Davis Woodstock, Vermont: Countryman Press: 2004. A useful traditional guide with lots of specific listings in its 333 pages, a portion of which is devoted to the Mohawk Trail.

Quiet Places of Massachusetts, by Michael J. Tougias, Edison N.J.: Hunter Publishing, 1996. A knowledgeable travel writers personal recommendations.

Trips and Trivia: An Architectural, Educational, Historical, and Recreational Guide to Western Massachusetts, by Linda K. Fuller, 1985. Crammed with ideas and insights.

The Mohawk Trail: Historic Auto Trail Guide, by Muddy River Press. Republication of 48-page classic.

History of Western Massachusetts (2 Volumes), by Josiah Gilbert Holland. Springfield MA: Samuel Bowles & Co., 1855. An early definitive study.

Early Settlement in the Connecticut Valley, by Peter Thomas, Stephen Innes and Richard I. Melvoin, Deerfield, Mass: Institute for Massachusetts Studies, 1984. A thorough review of the Valley's history.

Greenfield Gazette Centennial Edition, published February 1, 1892, on one the 100th anniversary of the newspaper. Discusses and illustrates each town and provides the essential history.

Greenfield, by Peter S. Miller and William C. Garrison, Images of America Series. Charleston, SC: Arcadia Publishing, 2000, 128 pages. An interesting, well-illustrated history of this important town.

Sermons in Stone: The Stone Walls of New England and New York, by Susan Allport. New York: Norton, 1990. A fascinating discussion of the types and uses of stone walls and related cultural structures.

A Long Deep Furrow: Three Centuries of Farming in New England, by Harold S. Russell. Hanover, NH: University Press of New England, 1976. A well-researched explanation of the changes in New England's agriculture.

Historic Collections, Being a General Collection of Interesting Facts, Traditions, Biographical Sketches, Anecdotes etc. Relating to the History and Antiquities of Every Town in Massachusetts, by John Warner Barber, Dorr, Howland & Co., Worcester, 1841. In addition to early descriptions of each town, this book contains 200 vintage engravings.

USEFUL CONTACTS

The Memorial Hall Museum Extensive information available online including descriptions of the area's Native Americans at memorialhall.mass.edu/home.html

Historic Derfield www.historic-deerfield.org

Franklin County Chamber of Commerce (413-773-5463), www.franklincc.org

Berkshires Visitors Bureau www.berkshires.org

Massachusetts Office of Travel and Tourism Information and a Guide at www.massvacation.com (1-800-227-6277)

The Visitors Center at I-91 Rotary & Route 2A on Miner Street in Greenfield (413-773-9393) offers free brochures and information. The complex sells maps, books and memorabilia.

Shelburne Falls Village Information Center (413-625-2544), 75 Bridge Street, Shelburne Falls. Open May through October daily, www.shelburnefalls.com

Massachusetts Country Roads www.masscountryroads.com provides local weather, lodging, dining and things to do in Western Massachusetts.

State Parks Brief descriptions and summary information on hiking, camping and fishing at www.masslive.com/outdoors/parks1.html

The Massachusetts Division of Fisheries and Wildlife (899-275-3474) www.mass.gov/masswildlife.org

The Rubel Bicycle Maps for Western Massachusetts and Central Massachusetts www.bikemaps.com/index.htm

The Virtual Birder www.birding.com/wheretobird/Massachusetts.asp

Massachusetts Birds: An Introduction to Familiar Species, by James Kavanagh, illustrated by Raymond Leung, Waterford Press. A handy laminated pocket guide

The Snowmobiling Association of Massachusetts (413-369-8092) www.sledmass.com

Mohawk Trail Association (413-743-8217) www.mohawktrail.com

Fishing the Deerfield River www.flyfishingconnection.com/deerfield.html

Massachusetts Maple Producers Association www.massmaple.org; Massachusetts Maple Seasonal hotline: 413-628-3912

Pick Your Own Sources at www.massgrown.org

Photo Credits

Jim McElholm

Cover Images
Fall foliage scene (back cover)

Book Images, listed by page

David J. McLaughlin

Cover Images
Bridge of Flowers in spring
  (front cover)
Tumbling water on the Mill River
  above Bissell Bridge (front cover)
Hail to Sunrise monument
  (back cover)

Book Images, listed by page

Patric duBreuil

ACKNOWLEDGMENTS

I am indebted to professional photographer Jim McElholm of Single Source Inc. (508-987-0809) in Oxford, Massachusetts, for the right to use his superb photographs. Patric duBreuil (866-561-7760), a Colrain photographer, gave us permission to use two of his images. Our book format does not do justice to his captivating panoramic images.

After the success of our first collaboration, it was an easy decision to partner again with Laren Bright in creating this book. His love of writing, his superb judgment and his zest for travel shaped the book in many special ways. This award-winning writer lives in the Los Angeles area and can be reached at 323-852-0433.

Cindy Wilson and her talented team designed the cover for *Along the Mohawk Trail* and did the interior design and layout of the book. Cindy, who lives in Saint Augustine, Florida, can be reached at 904-826-1672.

Many knowledgeable individuals helped us in our research. The staff at the Greenfield Community College, Amherst College, the Great Falls Discovery Center, the Pocumtuck Valley Memorial Association, the Shelburne Falls Village Information Center, the *Greenfield Recorder*, the Franklin County Chamber of Commerce, the Shelburne Falls Trolley Museum and the Carnegie Public Library were particularly helpful. The area's Historical Societies, Historical Associations and Historical Commissions provided invaluable advice and access; in particular, Marie Ferre (Northfield), Margaret Howland (Heath), Basil Hoffman (Colrain), Larry Carey (Warwick), Sue SanSuici and Jeff Singleton (Montague), and Tom Eisenman, formerly of Shelburne Falls. The Town Clerk of Colrain, Judith Sullivan, helped us track down the history of Colrain's covered bridges. Special thanks to Ann Banash of Greenfield Visitor center and Ann Hamilton of Franklin County Chamber of Commerce.

As always, my wife and daughter have supported me in this several-year effort to bring the unique attractions and beauty of another part of western Massachusetts to a broader audience. My daughter Devon has been particularly helpful in image selection.

David J. McLaughlin
Scottsdale, Arizona

ABOUT THE AUTHORS

David J. McLaughlin is a widely traveled writer and photographer with an abiding interest in New England. Dave was born in Boston, Massachusetts, and grew up in the central-western part of the state featured in this book. He is the author of five books and over forty articles on subjects ranging from motivation to medieval history.

Laren Bright is an Emmy-nominated, award-winning writer whose diversified writing career spans more than three decades. He has written extensively for television animation, working on staff at Hanna-Barbera and Warner Bros. Animation; co-published a magazine; written dozens of articles; and ghost-written three books.

ABOUT THE PHOTOGRAPHERS

Jim McElholm is the head of Single Source Inc. in Oxford, Massachusetts. Some of the images we have used are part of Jim's vast image databank, reflecting decades of New England photography.

Other images were commissioned by Pentacle Press for this book.

David J. McLaughlin contributed significantly to the collection of original images featured in this book. An accomplished travel photographer, Dave made seven photo trips to the Mohawk Trail area during 2003-2005. His collection of original photographs, *Images of the California Missions*, was published in 2003.

INDEX

OTHER BOOKS IN THE
Pathways to the Past Series

AROUND THE QUABBIN

Amidst the unrivaled natural beauty of Quabbin Reservoir's "accidental wilderness," where eagles now soar, are nestled magnificent 18th-century towns largely frozen in time. Stunning images and informative tidbits of history put you on the scene and guide you to this region's lesser-known places.

EXPLORING THE UPPER PIONEER VALLEY

From Deerfield, with its unparalleled collection of historic houses, through rich farming country settled by pioneers in the mid-1600s, to charming small towns, the Upper Pioneer Valley offers a variety of adventures to places out of the ordinary.